DATE DUE

ENERGY FOR THE FUTURE AND GLOBAL WARMING

SOLAR POWER

By ANNE ROONEY

Consultant: Suzy Gazlay, M.A.,
science curriculum resource teacher

Gareth Stevens
Publishing

Please visit our web site at: www.garethstevens.com
For a free color catalog describing Gareth Stevens Publishing's
list of high-quality books, call 1-800-542-2595 (USA) or
1-800-387-3178 (Canada).

Library of Congress Cataloging-in-Publication Data available upon
request from publisher.

ISBN 978-0-8368-8403-6 (lib. bdg.)
ISBN 978-0-8368-8412-8 (softcover)

This edition first published in 2008 by
Gareth Stevens Publishing
A Weekly Reader® Company
1 Reader's Digest Road
Pleasantville, NY 10570-7000 USA

Copyright © 2008 by Gareth Stevens, Inc.

Produced by Discovery Books
Editors: Geoff Barker and Sabrina Crewe
Designer: Keith Williams
Photo researcher: Rachel Tisdale
Illustrations: Stefan Chabluk and Keith Williams

Gareth Stevens editor: Carol Ryback
Gareth Stevens art direction: Tammy West
Gareth Stevens production: Jessica Yanke

Photo credits: DOE / NREL: / Robb Williamson cover, title page.
NASA: 5, 8, 27, 28. istockphoto.com: / Natalia Bratslavsky 10; /
Otmar Smit 15; / Alain Couillaud 24. Library of Congress: 12. Sandia National
Laboratories: / Randy Montoya 18, 19. The Solar Cooking Archive / solarcooking.org:
21. SOLON AG: 22. University of Texas at El Paso: / Dr. Huanmin Lu 23.

Printed in the United States of America

1 2 3 4 5 6 7 8 9 11 10 09 08 07

CONTENTS

Cover photo: The Adam Joseph Lewis Center for Environmental Studies at Oberlin College, Oberlin, Ohio, uses solar panels on its roof. Most of the power for the building's energy needs comes from the solar panels.

Words in **boldface** appear in the glossary or in the "Key Words" boxes within the chapters.

CHAPTER ONE

ENERGY AND GLOBAL WARMING

When you walk, run, or ride your bike, your body uses energy that you get from food. Food is your body's fuel. Your body burns up food to make energy. It uses that energy to keep warm and to do things.

In a similar way, we burn **fossil fuels** to create heat and power. Fossil fuels are coal, oil, and natural gas. These fuels formed in the ground over millions of years. Today, most of our energy comes from fossil fuels.

The demand for energy

The world's demand for energy is increasing. The growing number of people means more energy is needed.

Some countries and regions already use a lot of energy. Others are developing. China and India are **developing nations**. Their demand for energy is growing fast. They are building industries that need a lot of electricity. The people in developing nations are buying more vehicles that need gasoline. Almost all this energy comes from fossil fuels.

Fossil fuels are not **renewable**. Once they are used up, they will not be replaced. The world is using so much energy that people may someday use up all the fossil fuels. We need other sources of energy. One of these could be **solar** power — power from the Sun.

THE POWERHOUSE

All the planets and the Sun make up our solar system. The Sun lies at the center. It is bigger than all the planets combined. The Sun is also the source of energy for our solar system.

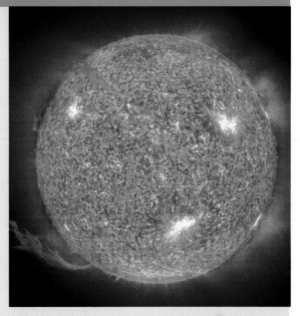

Deep inside the Sun, exploding gases release enormous amounts of energy. It takes one million years for this energy to reach the Sun's surface. Then, the energy begins its journey out into space. Most of that energy never falls on Earth.

Our planet is 1.3 million times smaller than the Sun. That mean only a tiny fraction of the Sun's energy reaches Earth. Still, on a cloudless day, Earth's surface receives enough solar energy to power all our homes and buildings. We are finding ways to use that power to help meet our future energy needs.

The Sun is a giant ball of super-heated, exploding gases.

> "Sun power is a pure gain to humanity. It subtracts nothing, the world will not be . . . [made poor] tomorrow by the fullest use of 'visible solar heat' today."
>
> C. H. Pope, author of *Solar Heat*, 1903

The fossil fuels we burn now formed long ago from plants and animals that used the Sun's energy to grow and live. The energy from those living things has been trapped underground for millions of years. When we burn fossil fuels, we release that energy.

Power from the Sun

Energy from the Sun is clean. It does not **pollute** (make dirty) air, water, or land. There is no waste. Solar power is renewable, which means it won't run out. Solar power is safe and quiet, too.

The Sun has always provided Earth with energy. Plants use energy from the Sun to grow. People and animals gain that energy when they eat plants. The energy we get from fossil fuels came from the Sun, too.

Carbon and carbon dioxide

All fossil fuels contain carbon. When we burn fossil fuels, carbon comes out of them. Carbon is an element, or basic substance. It combines with oxygen in the air to make the gas carbon dioxide.

Carbon is constantly reused. It goes around in a cycle. Plants use carbon dioxide to make fuel (or food) and oxygen. Animals and people eat plants for fuel and breathe oxygen in the air. They release carbon

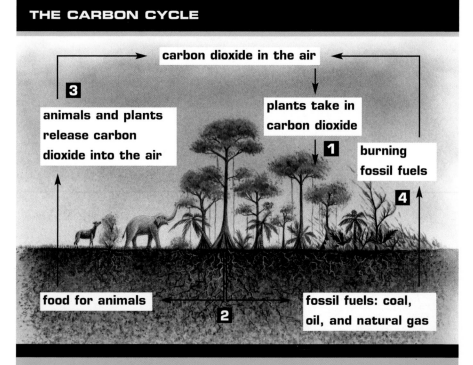

THE CARBON CYCLE

carbon dioxide in the air

3

animals and plants release carbon dioxide into the air

plants take in carbon dioxide

1

burning fossil fuels

4

food for animals

2

fossil fuels: coal, oil, and natural gas

Carbon is reused in a constant cycle. Plants take in carbon dioxide [1]. They make food for animals [2]. Animals and plants release carbon dioxide into the air [3]. We also burn fossil fuels and release carbon dioxide [4].

dioxide. The cycle works well as long as the amounts of carbon used and released are about equal.

In the past hundred years or so, more carbon dioxide than usual has been released. The cycle is out of balance. We burn huge amounts of fossil fuels every day, which makes a lot of carbon dioxide. We have also cut down forests and built on prairies. Fewer trees and other plants are left to remove carbon dioxide from the air. Today, the atmosphere contains more carbon dioxide produced by humans than ever before.

GLOBAL WARMING

The amounts of greenhouse gases in the air have increased in the last hundred years. Worldwide temperatures have risen by 1.1 degrees Fahrenheit (0.6 degrees Celsius) in the last hundred years, too. Scientists believe that the increase in greenhouse gases is changing the worldwide weather patterns, or climate. Climate change can cause global warming.

Violent storms are happening more often and are causing more damage. Hurricane Katrina (*white swirl, above left*) devastated New Orleans, Louisiana, and much of the Gulf Coast in August 2005. It was one of the strongest hurricanes to hit the U.S. in the last one hundred years.

Heating up

Carbon dioxide is a type of **greenhouse gas**. Water vapor and methane are other greenhouse gases. These gases in the air act like a

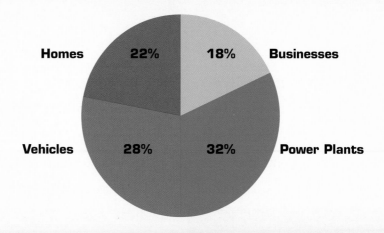

ENERGY USE IN THE UNITED STATES IN 2005

Homes 22% 18% Businesses

Vehicles 28% 32% Power Plants

This chart shows energy use in the United States. It shows how much was used by homes, businesses, **power plants**, and vehicles.

blanket. They keep the Sun's heat close to Earth to give us warmth. The warmth is necessary to life on Earth. If greenhouses gases increase, however, the world can get too warm. This effect is called **global warming**.

We can reduce global warming by using fewer fossil fuels. To do this, we need to turn to other energy sources. Solar energy is one source.

KEY WORDS

global warming: the gradual warming of Earth's climate

greenhouse gas: a gas in the atmosphere that traps heat energy

pollute: to make land, air, or water dirty

renewable: having a new or reusable supply of material constantly available for use

CHAPTER TWO

ENERGY FROM THE SUN

For thousands of years, people have used light and heat from the Sun. Today, scientists are finding more ways to use solar energy for power.

The adobe (clay) walls of these houses in Taos Pueblo, New Mexico, heat up and retain the Sun's energy well.

We can trap and use light and heat that reach Earth from the Sun. It is easy to transfer (move) heat. We use solar heat to warm buildings or heat water. We can use it right away, or we can store it for later use. For example, solar panels collect the Sun's heat. The solar panels can also use the Sun's heat to make electricity.

Passive solar power

There is a very simple way to use energy from the Sun. We can let its warmth and light fall onto objects or buildings. This process is called passive solar power. Passive means still, or not moving. Passive solar power uses no moving parts.

HOW HEAT MOVES

Heat moves in three ways:

1. Heat is a kind of **radiation**. It gives off energy in rays, or waves. Solar heat travels through space by radiation. Another name for solar radiation that reaches Earth is "heat."

2. Heat can transfer from one object to another by **conduction**. If you touch something warm, conduction carries the heat to your hand. You can burn yourself.

3. Heat passes through liquids and gases by **convection**. As a gas or liquid heats up, its particles move around. Hot particles rise. Colder particles sink. Many solar power systems use convection to make electricity.

People have always used passive solar power. They built houses with windows that face south. South-facing windows and walls get the most sun. Windows let in heat and light. Thick walls absorb plenty of heat. They heat slowly during the day. At night, the walls slowly release their heat to keep the building warm. Walls heated all summer long release heat during the winter.

Active solar power

Active solar power systems have moving parts. Pumps or fans send the heat to where it is needed. Solar panels can collect the energy. Simple solar panels are solar **thermal** (heat) collectors. They are often used to heat water or buildings. The solar panel contains a set of pipes holding a liquid. The dark panel absorbs heat from the Sun. It passes the heat to the liquid in the pipes. The hot liquid is pumped to a water tank. The liquid does not

MARIA TELKES (1900–1995)

Maria Telkes was born in Budapest, Hungary. She first became interested in solar power at school. Telkes studied science and then moved to the United States to research solar energy. In 1948, she designed an active solar heating system. The system was for the Dover Sun House in Dover, Massachusetts. It was the first solar-powered house in the United States. Telkes also invented a solar-powered system for life rafts. It made drinking water from seawater. She invented a solar oven, too.

Maria Telkes was one of the first scientists to devise ways to use solar energy. This picture was taken in 1956.

SOLAR POWER

GOOD THINGS	PROBLEMS
Unlimited supply in hot, sunny regions	Limited supply in colder, cloudy regions
Clean energy	Some solar power plants need large areas of land to collect energy.
Renewable	Depends on weather patterns Does not work at night
Many possibilities for future uses	Fossil fuels are used to make and run some solar collectors.
Silent	Systems can be expensive

come out of the pipes. Heat from the liquid passes through the walls of the pipes to warm the water in the tank. This process is called heat exchange. The liquid from the panels is then pumped back to the panels to be heated again.

The hot liquid can also heat a concrete block or a floor. Solar panels can provide heat for a single building. Sometimes, many panels are linked together to serve a whole community.

KEY WORDS

conduction: the movement of heat or electricity by direct contact

convection: the movement of heat by circulation in a gas or liquid

radiation: energy given off as invisible waves and particles

thermal: having to do with temperature or heat

CHAPTER THREE

ELECTRICITY FROM SUNLIGHT

It is easy to use the Sun's energy to heat water and buildings. But we need energy for other work, too. We need power to run machines in factories and appliances at home. To make this power, we must change heat energy into something else.

Making electricity

Energy from the Sun is primary (basic) energy. Electricity is a secondary source of energy. It is called secondary because it is made from something else. We can convert heat and light from the Sun into electricity.

We have seen how simple solar panels collect heat. There is another kind of solar panel. It has no water pipes running through it. Instead, it is a group of compartments, or cells. These are **photovoltaic (PV) cells**. "Photo" means light. "Voltaic" means electricity. The cells are able to turn light into electricity. The electricity can be used right away. More often, it is stored and used when needed.

Photons

Light contains tiny packets of energy, called **photons**. When a photon hits a surface, its energy can be freed. Energy from the photons doesn't simply disappear. It turns into another type of energy.

Think of catching a ball. The ball has energy to move through the air. When the

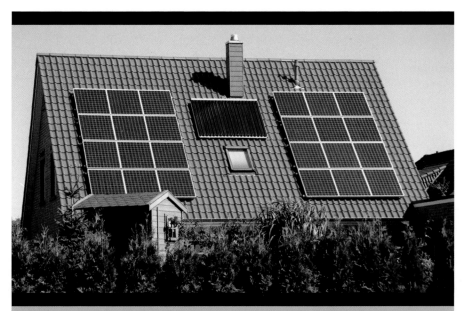

Houses with solar panels can use the Sun's energy for heating and for producing electricity.

ball hits your hand, it pushes your hand backward a little, and your hand heats up a tiny bit. The energy that moves and heats your hand was transferred from the moving ball.

A similar thing happens when energy from photons turns into other kinds of energy. Light energy from the photons makes electricity inside a PV cell.

Inside a PV cell

Most PV cells have a layer of silicon. Silicon is the second most common element (basic substance) on Earth. It is found in sand. Like all other substances, silicon is made of tiny parts called atoms. Atoms have parts called electrons. Moving electrons produce electricity. To do that, the electrons must first be freed from their atoms.

HOW A PV CELL WORKS

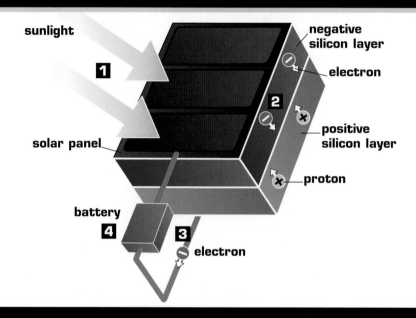

Sunlight strikes the solar panel [1]. Electrons are knocked out of the silicon. The negative silicon layer now has too many electrons. They move down toward the positive silicon layer [2]. Moving electrons make an electric current [3]. They charge the battery, which stores the power [4].

A solar panel frees up electrons. When sunlight hits the solar panel, some photons are absorbed, or taken into the silicon layer. Inside the layer, the photons' energy also knocks some electrons out of the silicon atoms. The electrons can then flow freely.

An electric field, or force, runs through the PV cell. This electric field causes all the freed electrons to flow in one direction. The flow of electrons is called an electric current, or electricity. The electric current can be taken from the PV cell and used right away or stored.

Just a few PV cells can power small things, such as watches and calculators. PV cells can also be put together to form whole systems. Many PV cells can work together in large panels. A lot of solar panels can produce huge amounts of electricity.

PV solar power plants

Today, most electricity made in power plants comes from fossil fuels. A few power plants make electricity from solar power, however.

There are several types of solar power plants. Some solar power plants use photovoltaic solar energy. They have a very large number of PV solar panels. The biggest solar plants are spread out over several square miles (kilometers). They collect and make energy for whole towns.

Thermal solar power plants

Other solar power plants use thermal solar energy. Thermal solar energy is energy created by the Sun's heat. Thermal solar power plants use solar energy to heat water and make steam. They make electricity with **turbines** and **generators** instead of PV cells. Turbines are engines with large blades that turn. Generators are machines that make electricity. A turbine works like a windmill. Instead of wind turning the blades, the force of the steam turns them. The turbine powers the generator.

Collecting the sunlight

There are several ways to collect the Sun's energy for thermal solar power plants. Today, three methods are used. The first is the solar trough (a long, shallow container). The second is the solar power tower (below). The third is the solar dish (opposite page). All three of these systems focus, or concentrate, the Sun's rays into a smaller area. The concentrated solar rays have even more energy.

The shape of a solar trough focuses the Sun's rays onto a pipe at the center of the trough. Oil in the pipe is heated. The hot oil is pumped to a power plant. There, it heats water in a second pipe to make steam.

A solar power tower collects the heat from thousands of mirrors placed at its base. The mirrors are placed so they reflect the Sun's rays to the top of the tower. Hot liquid in the

This solar power tower (center) is at Sandia National Laboratories in Albuquerque, New Mexico. It is used for solar energy research.

receiver

Solar dish mirrors in Albuquerque, New Mexico, focus the Sun's rays onto a receiver (left).

tower is piped to the power plant. The hot liquid in the pipes heats water to make steam for the turbine.

A solar dish concentrates the Sun's heat into its center. The **receiver** at the middle of the dish collects the energy. It can send the energy to make steam, like the solar trough does. Some dishes have small engines and generators attached. They immediately convert the solar heat into electricity.

KEY WORDS

photovoltaic (PV) cell: a device that turns light energy into electricity
generator: a machine that turns mechanical energy into electrical energy
turbine: a bladed engine powered by flowing fluid, such as moving air or water. A spinning turbine creates energy that can be turned into electricity.

CHAPTER FOUR

USING SOLAR POWER

Today, people use solar power to heat water and buildings. In some places, they use it for cooking. Solar energy is also used to make electricity. It can be used to make drinking water from seawater, too.

Where solar power is used

Only a small part of energy used in the world every day comes from solar power. But solar power is catching on. In 2005, $7.5 billion was spent worldwide on solar power. That amount was 40 percent higher than what was spent the year before.

Solar power works best in places with a hot, sunny climate. Many solar power plants are being built in California, Australia, and the Middle East. These regions receive a lot of sunshine.

Around the world

Germany does not always have sunny weather. But it makes good use of what sunlight it has. One of the world's largest solar plants is in Germany. It is the Gut Erlasse Solar Park in Arnstein. The PV cells in the Gut Erlasse Solar Park power plant produce 12 **megawatts** of electricity. This amount of power is enough for a town of nine thousand people.

Other nations are building much bigger solar power plants. A solar power plant in Victoria, Australia, will produce 154 megawatts.

COOKING WITH SOLAR ENERGY

Around the world today, millions of people do not have electricity in their homes. They cut down trees for firewood. People cook their food over wood fires. Whole forests are being lost in certain regions. Wood burning also increases greenhouse gases. It creates pollution, too.

Solar ovens are simple boxes. They trap the Sun's heat to cook food and heat water. Solar ovens, which use passive solar energy, can benefit people who burn wood for cooking. Fewer trees are cut down. People save money and time. The air is cleaner and healthier to breathe. Projects in Africa and South America show that solar ovens can help entire communities.

People in Bolivia make effective solar ovens from materials such as glass, aluminum foil, wood, and cardboard.

Gut Erlasse Solar Park in Arnstein, Germany, consists of many solar panels. The panels turn to follow the Sun as it moves across the sky.

A 100-megawatt plant is planned for Israel's Negev Desert. Later, it will be expanded to produce 500 megawatts. It will meet 5 percent of Israel's needs.

In the United States

The United States uses the second most solar power in the world. The amount of energy collected with PV cells in the United States was ten times more in 2005 than it was in 1995. Still, less than 1 percent of U.S. power comes from solar energy.

A very large solar power plant will be built just north of Los Angeles, California. It

SOLAR PONDS

A solar pond uses layers of saltwater to collect heat from the Sun. The saltiest water is heavier than plain water. It sinks to the bottom of the pond. The saltier the water is, the more heat it can store. The water at the bottom of the pond is hottest. Hot, salty water from the bottom of the pond is drawn off through pipes. The heat can be used to heat buildings. It can also make electricity. Solar ponds are cheap and easy to build. They are a good source of energy in countries with hot climates.

A solar pond collects and stores solar energy. This solar pond in El Paso, Texas began working in 1986. It is no longer used for solar energy research.

"As the technology for solar cells gets better and better, this form of clean, renewable energy will find more applications that take up less space and produce more electricity, to meet the energy needs of our homes, schools and businesses."

Samuel W. Bodman, U.S. Secretary of Energy, July 14, 2005

This phone in a remote region of the Middle East is powered by solar energy.

will cover 4,500 acres (1,821 hectares). The plant will have twenty thousand solar dishes. Each one will be 37 feet (11.3 meters) across. The dishes will focus heat onto engines that will produce electricity.

By 2012, the dishes will produce 500 megawatts of electricity. This amount of power is enough for a city of about three hundred thousand people.

Solar power at home

Solar panels can be fitted to the roof of any kind of building. More and more people are adding solar panels to their homes. They often save money on energy bills. These people also want to use clean, renewable energy.

Fitting solar panels to homes can be expensive. Even in hot, sunny regions, not many homes use solar power yet. But solar panels are starting to get cheaper. In some places, new homes are being built with solar panels. New solar panels will use the collected energy to supply electric light as well as heat.

Power in remote places

You may have seen solar lights that some people use to light walkways outside their homes. The photovoltaic (PV) cells in the solar lights convert sunlight to electricity. The electricity is stored to use when it starts to get dark. The lights don't need any cables or outside wires to connect them to an electricity supply.

Solar power is useful for other devices that don't have a power supply. Road signs light up at night with solar power they collect in the daytime. Phone booths in remote areas can run on solar power.

KEY WORDS

megawatt: a unit of measurement for power. One megawatt is one million watts. Electrical energy is measured in units called joules. One watt is the same as one joule per second.

CHAPTER FIVE

A SUNNY FUTURE

What part will solar power play in our future? It will provide a good supply of electricity in sunny regions. New inventions will make solar power cheaper. Engineers are making solar panels using new materials. The panels are thinner and more powerful than silicon panels. They will make it easier to use solar power.

Helping poorer nations

Countries in Africa and southern Asia have plenty of sunshine. Many of these countries are poor, but their energy demands are growing all the time. Developing nations could meet their future energy needs using solar power. The developing countries would not need to rely on fossil fuels.

SOLAR FABRIC

Researchers have developed a solar fabric. The fabric contains a network of tiny solar cells woven into the material. Metal threads in the fabric carry the solar energy to a battery for later use. The solar fabric can be draped anywhere. The U.S. Army has used solar fabric for tents. The tents provide power for computers, lighting, and cooling systems in "the middle of nowhere."

SPACE POWER

Solar-powered vehicles have been used in space for many years. Spacecraft traveling near the Sun often use solar power. Space vehicles sent to explore Mars use power from solar panels to travel the surface of the Red Planet.

Some countries plan to build solar power plants in space. **Satellites** orbiting (traveling around) Earth or the Sun would collect solar energy. They would beam it back to receivers on Earth. The solar energy would be converted to electricity. A Lunar Solar Power (LSP) system could provide a "power bridge" between the Moon and Earth. Sets of lunar solar panels would beam energy to receivers on Earth.

Cosmos 1 was launched as a test in 2005. It uses solar wind to move. This photograph shows Earth reflected in its sails.

Helios, the experimental solar-electric flying wing, was powered by solar energy. In 2003, it crashed into the Pacific Ocean near Kauai, Hawaii.

Many remote towns in developing nations have no electricity supply. Solar power can help these places most of all. Solar power could run plants that make clean water for drinking. It could provide refrigeration to keep food and medicines cool. Already, solar ovens and other small appliances are improving people's lives.

Sun-powered vehicles

In the future, there will be cars and boats powered by the Sun. Australia holds a race for solar-powered cars every year. A solar-powered ferry will soon travel between San Francisco and Alcatraz Island in California. In the future, there will be solar-powered trains. Already, there are spacecraft using solar winds. *Cosmos 1* was the first solar sail spacecraft to be tested.

Solar power's future

A single source of power will not meet all our energy needs. But solar power will play an important role in our future energy needs. It will be combined with other renewable energy sources, such as wind and water. Solar power will help make hydrogen gas for cars.

Hydrogen, like electricity, is a secondary source of energy. All these forms of energy will provide us fuel for the future that is safe and clean.

KEY WORDS

developing nation: a country that is in the process of building its industries. These countries usually have fast-growing populations as well. Many developing nations remain poor because they cannot feed all of their citizens and there aren't enough jobs.
receiver: a device that collects energy
satellite: an object that orbits (travels around) something else. Planets are satellites of the Sun. The Moon is a satellite of Earth. Other satellites are sent into space to orbit Earth. They can send signals back and forth.

GLOSSARY

conduction: the exchange of heat or electricity by direct contact

convection: the exchange of heat by circulation within a gas or liquid

developing nation: a country that is starting to build industries, or industrialize. These countries usually have fast-growing populations. Developing nations often remain poor because their populations are so large.

fossil fuels: fuels formed in the ground over millions of years, including coal, oil, and natural gas

generator: a machine that turns mechanical energy into electrical energy

global warming: the gradual warming of Earth's climate

greenhouse gas: a gas in the atmosphere that traps heat energy

photons: tiny packets of solar energy

photovoltaic (PV) cell: a device that turns light energy into electricity

power plant: a factory that produces electricity

radiation: energy given off as invisible waves and particles

receiver: a device that collects energy

solar: having to do with or coming from the Sun

thermal: having to do with temperature or heat

turbine: a type of engine powered by a flowing fluid. Turbines have large blades that spin, creating energy that can be turned into electricity.

TOP EIGHT ENERGY SOURCES

The following list highlights the major fuel sources of the twenty-first century. It also lists some advantages and disadvantages of each:

	Advantages	Disadvantages
Biofuels	renewable energy source; widely available from a number of sources, including farms, restaurants, and everday garbage	fossil fuels often used to grow the farm crops; requires processing facilities that run on fossil fuels in order to produce usable biofuel
Fossil fuels: coal, oil, petroleum	used by functioning power plants worldwide; supports economies	limited supplies; emit greenhouse gases; produce toxic wastes; must often be transported long distances
Geothermal energy	nonpolluting; renewable; free energy source	only available in localized areas; would require redesign of heating systems
Hydrogen (fuel cells)	most abundant element in the universe; nonpolluting	production uses up fossil fuels; storage presents safety issues
Nuclear energy	produces no greenhouse gases; produces a lot of energy from small amounts of fuel	solid wastes remain dangerous for centuries; limited life span of power plants
Solar power	renewable; produces no pollutants; free source	weather and climate dependent; solar cells expensive to manufacture
Water power	renewable resource; generally requires no additional fuel	requires flowing water, waves, or tides; can interfere with view; dams may destroy large natural areas and disrupt human settlements
Wind power	renewable; nonpolluting; free source	depends on weather patterns; depends on location; endangers bird populations

RESOURCES

Books

Parker, Steve. *Solar Power.*
Science Files: Energy (series).
Gareth Stevens (2004)

The Solar Car Book: A Complete Build-It-Yourself Solar Car Kit Including All the Parts, Instructions and Pain-Free Science.
Klutz, Inc. (2001)

Web Sites

www.eia.doe.gov/kids/energyfacts/ sources/renewable/solar.html
Visit the U.S. Department of Energy Web site for information about solar power and power plants.

solarcooking.org/plans/
Discover some easy plans for building your own solar oven for use anywhere!

Publisher's note to educators and parents: Our editors have carefully reviewed these Web sites to ensure that they are suitable for children. Many Web sites change frequently, however, and we cannot guarantee that a site's future contents will continue to meet our high standards of quality and educational value. Be advised that children should be closely supervised whenever they access the Internet.

INDEX